Shell Sho

Written by Deana Kirk
Illustrated by Tom Leonard

Modern Curriculum Press
A Division of Simon & Schuster
299 Jefferson Road, P.O. Box 480
Parsippany, NJ 07054 - 0480

Design and production by Kirchoff Wohlberg

ISBN: 0-8136-0798-1 Modern Curriculum Press

3 4 5 6 7 8 9 10 SP 01 00 99 98 97

Hermit Crab needed a new shell.

The shell she had was getting too small.

She found a shell.
But it had a hole in it.

5

She found another shell.
But it wasn't the right shape.

She found another shell.
But there was something in it.

She found another shell.
But it was too sharp.

She found another shell.
But it was near a shark.

9

She found another shell.
But it was too big.

She found another shell.
But it was too heavy.

11

She found another shell.
It looked fine.

But another hermit crab got it first.

At last, she found the right shell.
It was shiny and near the shore.

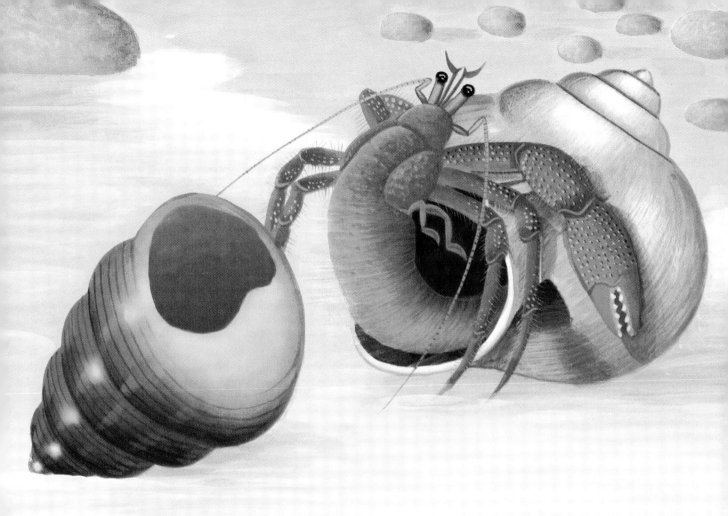

Hermit Crab walked out of her old shell.
Then she went into her new shell.

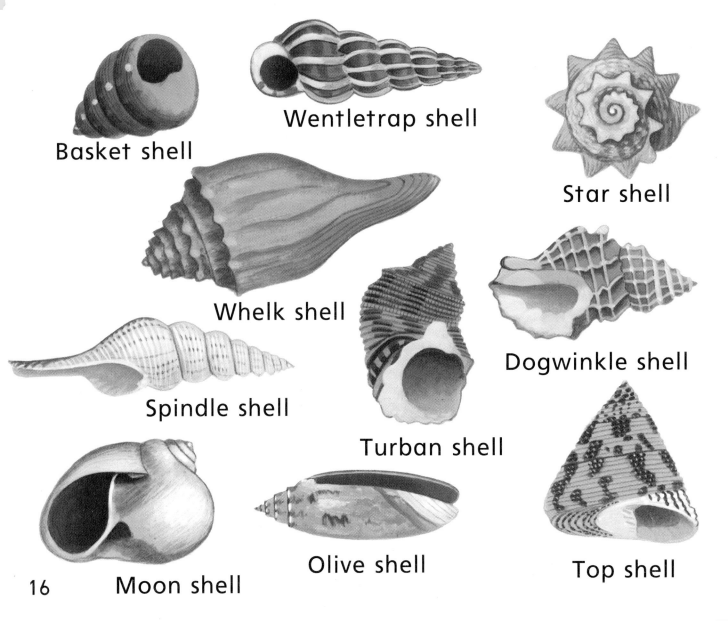

Basket shell

Wentletrap shell

Star shell

Whelk shell

Spindle shell

Dogwinkle shell

Turban shell

Moon shell

Olive shell

Top shell

16